To all who have caused my heartache,
And the disease that destroyed my body,
You all made me powerful like Taylor Swift
Therefore this book wouldn't exist without you
So I guess all that pain was worth it...

Most of all, thank you to the Hallmark Channel TV show THE
WAY HOME for inspiring me with their time-traveling pond. I
wouldn't have imagined it would create the theme of this poetry
book and make me love my local pond more.

CONTENTS

PONDERING REFLECTIONS

Poetry Book by Christina Vourcos

The pond might look innocent at first glance,
but its power is hidden within and
by the haunting of its Witch.
Her female rage has been shared with me.
I share her words. She has deemed these words
to be shared, through my transcription,
to compel you to reflect...
You will find in quick haste
the information you acquire...

POND JUMPING

What if you could jump into a pond
And head back in time, like a time machine,
Especially where you need to be?

Where would you go if you could?
What if the pond takes you
Where you don't expect?

What would you do?
What if it keeps you
Looking at its reflections?

What would you do?
It's time to figure out...

Part 1: Releasing The Unrequited

TIME: ENEMY OR LOVER?

Time, he is my enemy
He always rushes me
Even with my passions
But no matter what
He knows I need him
He has fragmented me
To wrap around him

Time, he is my lover
I can't live without him
He takes me on dates
As he strings me along
Because plays around
Every year, I expect more
He thrives in the unexpected

I want to walk away
Time knows he will win
He removes my chance
Of finding a partner, yet he
Keeps me happy with distractions

TIME, MY COMPANION

As the clock ticks to midnight
It's when I remember Time
He has shaped my life always
Like a constant companion
He's my knight, protecting
All my fragments of memories
And gathering all the musical notes
He signals a change within me
He connects me with the world
Seeming endless adventure
But it's a truly fragile illusion
As I dance through life while
Running desperately to passions
That will weave words together
Like a magical spell of healing
And investigating mysteries
Left unanswered, it may always be

MEETING THE MYSTERIES

They came in the night like mysteries
You want to unravel slowly like forbidden sweets,
But will they torture you when you least expect it
Or will you do it to yourself in their presence?

Who did you meet? Is he worth it?
Or someone who will lead you to hide?
Am I allowed to cry about the idea of him?
Or is he as guilty as sin in my mind?

Where could you meet? You're hidden
Deep levels where no one can find
Did you meet in my mind
Or somewhere around town?
Happy meetings aren't found here

CHILDLIKE WONDER

There was always something about nature
Like a belief that was magical, unique, and unexpected

So the adventures would lead to something new
led us to a special pond

We walked around like the place was ours
The trees were there as our guardians
The water with interesting creatures

A pond that would be something to reflect on
But I didn't know that then, that creating
Would give me a childlike wonder of life

Now I ponder if that pond is still there
Even though we're forever changed
Decisions and struggles that made us

Now I create with words with nature's power of time
Because I might never create a mini-me

PICK THE ANTI-HERO

What do you want, your anti-hero
The one who will do all that it takes
To be your equal partner in everything
Even if it means falling into the gray

You want to taste some kind of darkness
Without the consequences of your actions
You want to be part of my redemption

You need someone who balances
Every side of your personality
You can't help but pick the anti-hero

I'm what you want because of thrills
Make your everyday, adventures
And your fantasies come true
Pick your anti-hero who will make you
Feel all your passions deep within
I will make you feel like a queen

CRYING AT THE GYM

If I can't have you, I'll lose myself instead
Like a ghost wandering around
Nothing would make a difference

I was staring at the sky, expecting you
Why would I stay there believing in you?
Your friends would say I'm insane for this

I was in love with you, and you can't tell me
About being sad because you taught me
You can't tell me you feel bad about it

I wish you could be afraid of me
I would crash your parties in town
Because I thought it was my chance
To explore the hidden mysteries I could photograph
To prove that your loss is now legendary

SECOND CHANCE?

I dreamt of a second chance
We would be older and wiser
Maybe somehow see me as yours

You will notice how you impacted
Every aspect of my life, and I realize
That you should have asked me before

We would finally find moments together
We would be united with letter-writing
We would have things in common

Or maybe I would find out that someone
That I didn't know was interested in me
Now we could finally be together

Or maybe I would have a second chance
To tell you that I was better off without you
If I could jump into the pond, would it change?

MIND GAME

I always wanted someone to challenge me
Someone clever but secretly kind to others

He would find me a puzzle and be a puzzle for me
He could unlock my mind and
I would be a part of his mind

We would solve cases together even the fictional
He would push me to my limits
We would achieve brilliance

An endless mind game
He would be sassy with everyone
It would make every day an adventure
But maybe like superheroes

He would only be fictional
In my mind game

LIKE THE SMALLEST MAN

I never wanted you, but you made me
Believe that I should, no matter how I hated you
For haunting me for some kind of attention

You had control of my actions
You loved it when I could be
Your actress on your stage

Even after all this time, I still hate you
For lingering in my mind and broke me with your lies
No matter what I want, no matter the hate
You made me want to believe in redemption

You were supposed to be my "enemy to lover"
You couldn't even be friends with me, truly
You were just laughing behind my back
I still want to get you back for damaging me

If I could, I would protect myself from being in your orbit
I tried to forgive you, and you laughed

IT'S SO HIGH SCHOOL

I was supposed to find my first boyfriend
Instead, I fell again for someone unattainable
He would leave for college with dreams
That didn't include me with him

I spent my time waiting for a chance
Left alone to imagine what could have been
So much that I couldn't notice anyone
Did I lose my chance somehow then?

All was fine because I had my friends
That made me believe that they would stay
I know I wouldn't jump into the pond
No matter the fun I had, the interests
That stayed with me for years after

I want someone who makes me feel so high school
The feeling that I learned from stories
But the drama was just as expected

COLLEGE GUY IN THE BAND

Growing up, I didn't understand why
The girls wanted someone with royal pains
All for their chance to be powerful
Like pretty heels that hurt with time

I wanted the sweet musician
Who knew how to write music
That had some deep feelings
That could change my life

As I grew older, I wanted a college guy
Who would rock the stage with his band
Who could orchestrate the audience
Who would tap into my passions
Who would change my life

But no matter what I did
The college guy didn't seem to care
If I could turn back time
I wouldn't let him make me a ghost waiting
For the college guy in the band

SO LONG, ANTONIO

If I could jump back to when I left
To my first friend, first heartbreak
I loved this place for so long, it was my home
You taught me of magical adventures

Would you keep the secret of time travel?
What would I learn now, going back?
I already know that home isn't the same
Second chances didn't work
Because my heart can't let go

Even the cancer didn't bring us back
I've gone through the hardest time in my life
I wonder what I should have done differently
If I let you go years ago, my first unrequited love

Would I have a different life with someone else?
Instead of being me without the love of my life
All I have left is a legacy of the written word

HE HATES ME, HE LOVES ME

He hates me, doesn't he?
Time, he has been unkind
I took a fragment of my youth
When my health was unwell
As soon as I realized
He took even my healing
But he loves, doesn't he?
Time has been kind,
Gave me plenty of fragments
Filled with unadulterated passion
As soon as I realized
I couldn't live without him

LEFT BEHIND

When you didn't want me as a partner,
I grew to be who I thought you wanted
I found what you enjoyed, so I could enjoy it
I looked for all the chances to speak with you

None of it was enough, no matter how much
Everyone told me that I needed to give up
Yet I'm reminded of the moments that
Everyone tells me that I gave up
But it wasn't you until I broke down

When you still didn't want me,
I decided to become a version of myself
The one who shares the knowledge
The job that distracted you from what you wanted
When you discard that version,
It became everything I had always wanted

ARE YOU NEEDED?

I can't find who I am with you
But I realize now that I led you to
Become the sun when all this time
I needed clouds to guide me

You didn't see me tortured
Being in your presence
Because no matter what you tried
You didn't care enough for me
I only need the idea of you

I don't even know what I need,
But I know it isn't any of the guys
Who have I broken my own heart for?

But I need you, yes, you
The one that will change my life
And I won't wish for any more but
How do I convince you when you're not here

BLOOMING?

Everything is blooming
But I don't feel like I am
Pain consumed me
Stuck at Winter while you're Spring
Tired of the consistent drought
Even if it's rained a bit recently
When do I start to grow again?
Why does it feel like it's slow?
Maybe blooming takes time
But we don't see it passing by
Or looking too closely at it
We need a quick time-lapse
Maybe I'll believe that it's real
Maybe I'm blooming in the pain
You don't feel like I have

MET MY SELF FOR TEA

Inspired by Jennae Cecelia's poem
"I Met My Younger Self For Coffee"

I met my younger self for tea
She asked me what tea to brew
I knew then that it was a test—
Which tea would "future me" pick?

She shares her worries about
Losing her muse of unrequited love
I tell her that she keeps her muse
And adds another much-needed
Once we have our tea in cups
Both chai tea with soy milk
I tell her that Poetry saves us

We say goodbye with a hug
Telling her that I'm proud
But I'm thankful that
She still trusts a hug
It's a way to hide our face
We survived cancer

"MOVE ON" TEA

If only there were a tea to move on
I would drink it to let go of the past
Just enough to reduce the pain
While remembering the lessons
While picking the right memories
It would take a fortnight to take effect
Would it be worthwhile to take?

YOU GIVE UP ALL THE TIME

If I give up so easily, why do I keep trying?
If I give up so easily, why have I survived?
It's not about bravery, or lack of it,
It's about being you despite all of it
It's about sharing the best of yourself
It's about taking care of ourselves
It's a way forward, it's why I keep trying
Different ways to make the best changes

FALLING FROM CLOUD 9

Falling from Cloud 9 for far too long
I'm letting go of what I hoped for love
I'm losing sleep falling from Cloud 9
The story feels over now, losing myself
And everything I could have had, I lost
Castles are crumbling as I try to hold on
I wish I knew all of what I know now
But it wouldn't ever change at all
It's always been written in the stars
As I fall with a self-made broken heart

THE SONG ON THE RADIO

I heard a song on the radio
One I hadn't heard in a long time
And it made me laugh when I realized
I still preferred the cover you did years ago
It is still one of the best things you left me
It wasn't even one of your originals
Now I realize that I have become a poet
Believing it would lead me to the songwriter
I grew up believing would be my perfect match
But it wasn't true, I needed poetry despite you

LEFT BEHIND

The one you left behind
When you didn't want me,
I grew to be who I thought you wanted
When you didn't want me,
I decided to become
a version of yourself
that you discarded, but it was everything
I had always wanted

AFFIRMATION

Let the time be, let the time be,
Let everything I can't change find its way,
May I find compassion in this world,
Once, when I was a chica, I looked up
At las estrellas and saw the universe,
and knew I was made of more,
I am an estrella made of so much more

YOU'RE THE REASON

Wonder why the water returns to Earth?
The patch of space behind the sun,
And the heat, the kitchen is in smoke, sear
Your hands bloomed around my heart,
A soft tongue breaks the bone...

But of the epitaph: Here lies a woman
Crushed and purple under some tirade,
Brushing her teeth with crystals,
She wonders why the water returns
To the Earth, the city rises up
In all the lights to meet you,
The underbelly of a sandcastle,
The patch of space behind the sun,
The roads we choose

IT HAPPENS LATE

It happens, even late, the fight for love,
The light breaking through the dark,
The candles are lit through our power,
Stars gather our dreams and pour them into ponds,
Send up our words into the bitter cold air,
This late, the bones of the body flare,
And tomorrow turns into a ticking clock

I watch as he stirs sugar into my tea
He sets the spoon down and lifts
My cracked cup to his lips
His eyes poke through my soul
As he waits to see what I will do next

Only in my dreams do I see
Romantic things done for me
If I had one night left on Earth
I would be intimate with books
My favorite character worships all of me

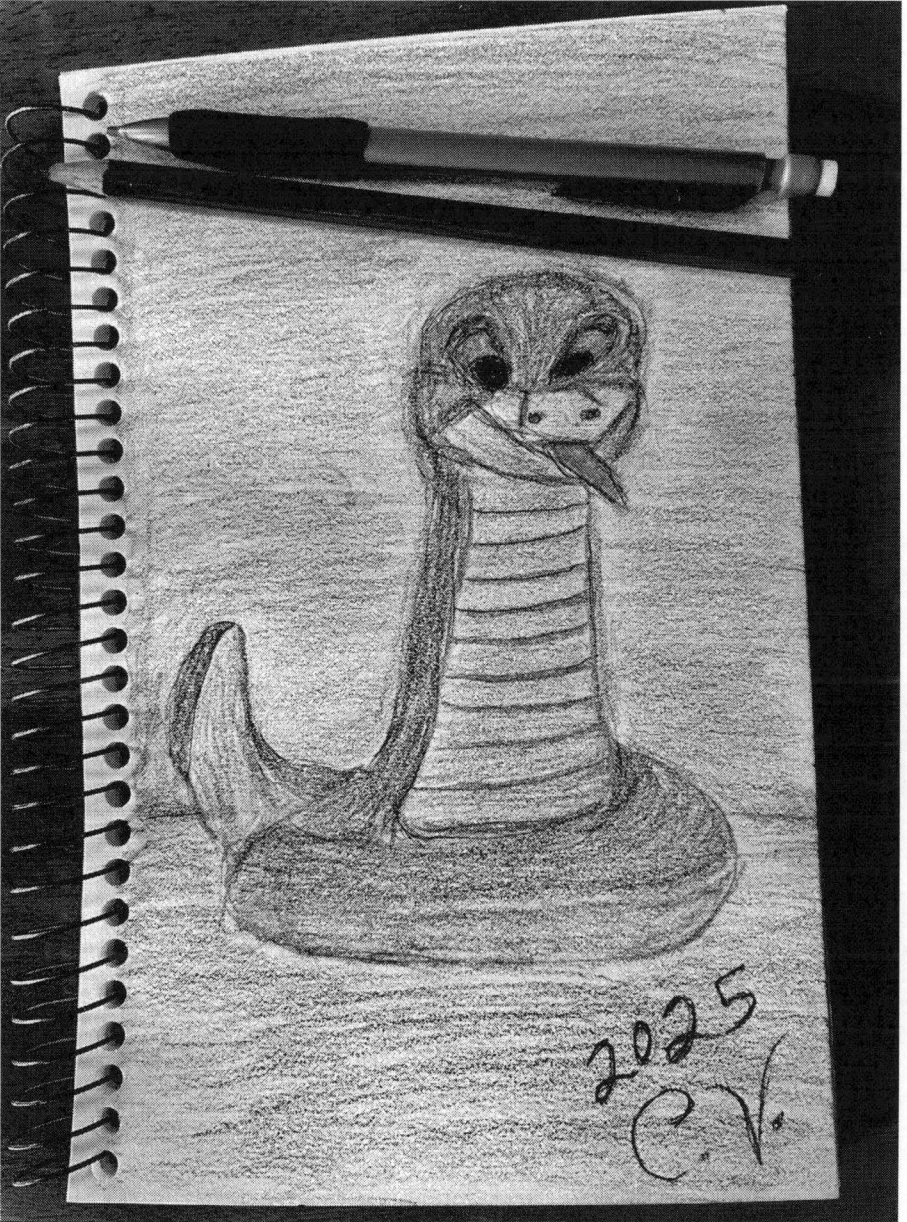

SKIPPING RECORD

You're a record on repeat if I keep listening
I'll understand why things are the way they are
Maybe I can find you beyond those words
That keeps repeating to me a million times

Will it help to find a solution to the repetition
Of the beat deep within our bodies
Especially if you have made me
Miserable, treating me as invisible

You repeat over and over as if
It could be important, but I know you
There's no chance that you could be worthy
No matter what, you keep reminding me
You're the record I want to skip
No matter what happened in my mind

ENDLESS MUSIC

You're the music I keep listening to
Because it inspires the words on the page
But why can't I make my day better? Why do I need you?
Do I need something special every day?
If so, could I find it somewhere else? Or something new?
Do you make my day better, or is this what I imagine?

I know you make my day better
because you find ways to make me smile when I'm tired
You make my day better because you support me
When I need it the most, even if it's every day, you're there
Your words matter because they make my day better
I can't live without the endless notes

You're a memory that I can't let go of
Because I believed you made my day better, now I have to

LAUGHING ECHO

The sound of crackling fire in the cold night,
A reminder that happiness can suddenly disappear

Maybe your laugh echo can be the joke
A laugh that sounds like
someone clever at the moment
A laugh that is like a green apple,
sweet and sour, like a grey rebel

Do you like my laugh, or do you say that?
I want to like your laugh, but
I worry your jokes will backfire
Do I like your laugh or
that you're happy with me?

Can I trust your laugh?
I want to trust your laugh,
but I always expect it's at me, don't I?

THE FAMILIAR

He is the cat that wanders
But remains my familiar
He tells me the line, "You seem familiar,"
But his smirk suggests that it is his way
To speak with me, if only I could believe
He wants to know who I am
Or just a pretty face ready to destroy

I saw him in my dreams, he filed through my memories
But when I saw him there in the cafe
I couldn't say he looked familiar
Maybe he remembers when he says,
"You seem familiar," but before I can ask
He disappears into the crowd

Why did he say, "You seem familiar?"
Do I remind him of the girl he ignored years ago?
What changed, me or him? Will you answer that?

SPENT NIGHTS

I know now that I couldn't spend
One more night with you
Never interested in more
Like long nights chatting
Or spending time reading together
Even if it's different books

But it doesn't matter, the idea of you is fictional
Like a favorite character, I've read before
If I spent my life with you,
It would cost more than can I afford
Will it be worth spending it all?
As I've looked back,
It would be best to spend it all
On all kinds of books

Where can I get what I want
Even an unexpected ending
Or the realistic, sad ending

HEART BREAKS

Do you hear my heart breaking?
Because I keep saying "I love you"
To the boys who never saw me
As worthy as others in their minds

I'll never trust myself to say "I love you"
Because it leads to losing the game
Of believing anything is possible

I'm waiting to hear the words
"I love you" from a guy who truly believes
I want to scream "I love you" as if the sound
It will change how you feel about me

The girl says to the boy,
"I love you" but all she receives is
Silence when the words are meant to repeat
It's only in the stories and the poems
Where we see the words,
But they are heartbreaks

THINKING OF YOU

When I think of you, I realize
I'd rather see my favorite indie band than yours
They usually perform far away, mind you
When I think of you, I realize
I want the guy who knows British slang
And I know more Spanish, mind you
When I think of you, I realize
I want a guy who can chat about reading
You should have been able to, mind you
When I think of you, I realize
I don't miss you, I miss your world
I can have my adventures, mind you
When I think of you, I realize
You don't make me cry anymore
But I'm glad I met you, mind you

TAKING CARE OF YOU

The leading man says, "I'll take care of you,"
And I will believe it because his actions
Like the blanket placed on me
When I say I am cold
That's when I know

I want to hear the words
"I'll take care of you"
More than "I love you"
Do you care enough
To notice when I need your help

Would you care without prompting
Or do you need reminders?
It's hard to believe
I want to care about you,
But I need you to care more about me

HALF OF A WHOLE

You aren't my half of a whole
We should be equals working together
Why is something missing
Shouldn't I be complete?
I am single and independent
Could I have more, yes,
But we all want more

"You complete me"
It's a man's belief that
A woman can not exist
Without them but we exist
Without tying a knot with another

You don't complete me
If you did, I wouldn't be
The woman that I am,
Stronger than ever
Overcoming challenges
So why do I not feel complete?

BEAUTIFUL FLAWS

I'd say our flaws are beautiful,
But it would be a lie
Our flaws have hurt everytime
Even when we don't even try

That we can't see our faults
No matter how hard we try
But go ahead, say that they are beautiful
Just like your flawless face I'll imagine
The words said by one of my favorite actors

Are our flaws like scars that don't go away
Or something that changes like the weather
I want to believe our flaws as beautiful as the stars
Because that means our work is worthwhile

How do you define beautiful, my darling?
Is it like nature during a hurricane
Or when you spend a rainy day at home?
Where are your flaws?

YOUR BAD DAYS

Will I love me even on my bad days?
More likely than you or anyone else
That could be my lover

Only bad boys in fiction are ready for redemption
With grey vibes could only say
"I will destroy anyone who hurt you"
Because these bad boys can handle
My darkness held within

Would you let me break
All the plates that you have
So I can let go of all the bad
In my days?

I won't believe you
Because I haven't seen it in my past
And for certain, not in the present

AM I RARE?

Rare? Like a first edition of your favorite book?
Like a record hard to find?
Am I that rare? Or have you not been near me?

Rare? Like a unique stone hidden deep?
Like interesting guys interested in me?
Or is that too rare?

Well, you will only find one of me
That's truly rare
I'm so rare that you'll
Never find someone like me, ever

WILL I BE LOVED?

You loved how I loved
Because I was devoted to you
Because I wanted to be the one
Who you worshipped
Even if it was ruining my life

But you never saw the bold pain
As long as I was there
Following Hades into the Underworld

You loved how I loved
Because it benefited you
Until I had enough
Your presence wasn't enough

You could have been my equal
But you never did enough for my heart
I walked away to fix myself

I DON'T LIKE ME

I don't like me when I am with you
You kept me silent until it was time
Treated me like obligation,
But it didn't feel real

I lost myself with you
But I saw the city as it should
I'll thank you for that

Just tell "past me" to leave
But I know I wouldn't
Because I wanted to feel something,
Even if it was heartache
Pain felt like living
Even when I didn't know pain

I don't like me because
Every guy I wanted didn't either, but
I found I love me more than them

FATED TO FALL IN LOVE

Was I fated to love those boys
Who would never love me back?
What a cruel joke to let me fall
Knowing I was breaking my own heart

Even though the lack of care
Push me away for a while to help me
But it truly was to help you

You made me fall in love
With the idea of you
So you could laugh
Like the best tortured comedy

You all wanted to be my friend
But you all wanted a dog
Someone loyal, who would always be there
Always coming back for more
Like wanting scraps fallen from the table

BREAKING MY OWN HEART

When I lose
It's always my fault
To break down like a car
Not picked up to drive

It is my failure
I chose this path
Like a choose-your-adventure story
But it always ends the same way

My heart is always broken
With every choice I make
You always make me this way

My heart breaks with my pen
When I decide to tell them my feelings
Knowing that they don't feel the same

HAVE I CHANGED?

It's like going to your former school
And flooded with memories at every turn
But broken by the things that were not there before

Yet the new feels like a better edition
To whom you were, so the broken feels like a shift
To a better time in the timeline

The familiar walkways tell me
I am home, but the new tells me
That you have lost, and so have I

But time will tell if you've changed
From the one I've met years before
This building's redesign

I wish I could see you again
Only to hear you say I've changed
Because that would be finally
My crowning achievement in your world

WHO AM I WITHOUT YOU?

When I said I didn't know me
Without you, I didn't realize
It means that I changed myself
But I will never lose myself
When it has never led to
A chance with someone like you

I know who I am
But you led me to
Make me something I didn't see
In the invisible moments
I've done it far too many times
Like the definition of insanity

You were trained this way
To lead women away
Don't believe me? Many have lost
Their languages and their cultures
Because men don't want
To lose their precious power

MY PERSONAL GHOST

You haunt me everywhere
The moments not good enough
You made me hollow version that
Could haunt you

Everything you did is a puzzle
That has a missing piece
In how you've changed me

You left me behind so easily
Because you never wanted
Who I am or who I could be
Everywhere there's something
That made me believe you could be
Worth the time

All the time spent was a loss
But now I can use you like
You used me, a benefit to our ultimate goals
Believe me, everywhere I look,
I find all that can be written into words

DO YOU UNDERSTAND?

No puedo entender
The words that ring in my head
I'm waiting for a moment
But others will say I don't know
Enough Spanish, or even worse
I don't know Español

How can I prove that I am
Latina enough to you
It hurts when I see others,
Who know what to say,
But no puedo entender
When even mi familia doesn't see
How much I try to prove
I haven't lost my roots to America

Maybe it's easier to fall for chicos americanos,
Those who don't care enough about me,
Chicos mexicanos no pueden entender
That I am Latina enough, but they can't see it

NOT MEANT TO BE

It took a fortnight to realize
That some things aren't meant to be
"We aren't meant to be" have haunted me
Who needs horror movies when you've hurt
Being cruel, laughing when I couldn't see
We weren't meant to be

Time has passed, but your kindness
Is not speaking to me
Letting me know I closed a door
But the window is still open
To remind me of the sandbox
Filled with adventures long ago

I can imagine your dark expression
Telling me that we could be fiction
Even that wasn't possible
I'm alone because of you
But I am to blame

THE WORDS I'VE HEARD

Lo siento, I'm sorry I've heard it
I've said it, it pains me knowing
I'm not good enough

If you hear me say I'm sorry
I have questioned everything
If you say to me I'm sorry
I wonder what I've done

Lo siento, I'm sorry
We say it so much
Out of worry, rarely
Because we've done wrong
We've been made this way

If we have done wrong
"I'm sorry" isn't good enough
Just words, echoes until we see:
Kneeling on the ground,
And some action of change
I am sorry, lo siento

CAN WE FIX THIS?

What is this we're trying to fix?
Maybe we missed crossing paths
Or we didn't notice each other

Is it too late for us to meet?
Can we fix this?
Maybe we weren't meant to be
So we can't fix this distance

It's too late for you to change
Your mind, if you picked someone else
If you've hurt me
I can give you chances
How do you know if it's too late?
You'll know, you can't fix this

Is it too late for me to fix this?
I've wondered each day
Have I lost my chance?
Did I miss my perfect match?
Or do I need a matcha?

LETTING YOU GO

I let go by falling in love with someone else
Someone who also doesn't see me
It's like falling in love with a British actor
You're just an American who doesn't know him

It's okay, I don't love you anymore
But I think of you alongside
All the boys who never loved me
Including famous actors and singers
You're not special, just one of many

Why do I miss guys not worth my time?
They are distant memories
You all have changed after all
You all aren't who I fell for
I hate that you all changed without me

Maybe you all didn't change, maybe I did
I lost the glasses that made me see you all as special
So why am I here reviewing memories
At this seemly peaceful pond

WHO IS AT FAULT?

When everything is lost
We want to give fault
But it isn't always someone's fault

You could go back in time
But nothing changes, no matter what
So, who is at fault?
Have we lost every moment
When we walk away

I wish I could hate you
Or something you've done
But you couldn't change anything
Just like I couldn't
You I know how determined I am
When my heart is involved

If nothing can change in the past
Why look there when the future is waiting
If it's no one's fault, what do I do to move to the future

WHAT'S BETTER THAN OKAY?

I wish I could say that all will be resolved
I wish I could say that it will be okay
But I don't think I can ever say

I can't predict the future
Even with cards
So, how can I say
It's going to be okay
This is what I do know
Whatever okay means
We've gone through the worst
And the best I can say
We have done everything

"It's going to be okay" are the words
We say to try to give each other hope
But it might not be the words you need
Why do we use the word "okay"?
Even though we know that not everything
Will be better than okay

MISSING IT ALL

You tell me an adventure
With your posh accent
You bring intrigue

You keep me balanced
You make me lose it
You're the monster willing to change
You're in my dreams, flying to me
But when I wake, you're missing

I see you in pictures and stories
Your blond hair whispering in the air
Your body fit like the god of the underworld
Tempting to touch that I could die from

Never say I don't care enough
As I wait for you, from dawn to dusk
I need your banter, passion, and cleverness
You're my partner, and I am your crime
So, do you miss me? You're my mystery

TEARDROPS OF POISON

Should I have let you tear my heart
So much that I cried tears of poison
Am I allowed to cry in front of you?

I see you now, and it still hurts
I think of the ways you laughed
About all the crazy things you said I did
But did I really? Or was it in your head?

I was just someone that you could push
To cry on cue, I'm tired of you
Stuck in my mind that I'd rather replace
You with my favorite anti-hero redeemed at the end
He is everything you couldn't be

Tell me that I'm in your mind tonight
And I made you cry all last night
You'll see what you did to me years ago
You'll cry like the man told to keep it all in
The teardrops will be your poison

A MEMORY NOT FORGOTTEN

May their memory be a blessing
Some say to provide comfort
Día de los Muertos for us to never forget
Those who have passed on
But what about those who are still alive
Just not in our lives for God knows why

Those memories are stuck like a file
That can't be retrieved from a filing system
The filing system in my mind keeps you there
As if you were valued history
That must not be deleted

I can't let your memory leave me
You're tied to far too much to swipe away
Go ahead, find your presence within me
Deleted it with a swipe of a key
Your discarded computer that was sent off
To someone else to figure out

A MISSING DAY

I don't miss that day that I met you
I don't miss that day you told me the truth
That I meant nothing even though you knew
I was something
I don't miss that day you made me
The version you wanted

I think of you, but I don't miss that day
That I walked away from your so-called friendship
I would jump into a time-traveling pond to change
All the days that I lost following you and your silence

Tell me, right now
Do you miss those days when I worshiped you?
I'm sure you found someone to fill that well
The ducks on the pond foretell that day
When I realize that I miss what I believed
From the ripples from the rock you threw
But never changed who I would become

I LOST SLEEP

Those girls who say they lost sleep without him
That's cute, but they haven't had a job
That takes your self-worth each day
Anxiety all night, to repeat it all again
To the point where you have to leave
Or maybe it's him all over again
Not truly seeing our worth
To the point where you have to leave
But they say they lost sleep over him
Did they end up in the hospital after chemo
Because you were hand signing in delirium
Believing you solved a true crime mystery
Where was the guy who would solve it with us?
We lost more than sleep, even without him

STUCK IN THE PAST

You think you're special, haunting me,
Never believed that I could be
Anything more than your joke
To your interested crowd

The same day you broke me with your lies
You took your religion and threw it
As your shield to damage me

Now, when I've lost faith
You haunt me through your religion
Every holy day is a reminder
Of how I can't let what you did go
When my religion says I should forgive

I'm part of the tortured poets
Because you started the torture
Before I knew what torture meant
The pain that won't let go, no matter what
You found a way to keep me in the past

LONE STAR RISING

If you knew you would be
The lone star rising in the sky
Above the pond's horizon
No other stars rising beside you
Not even one star nearby

Rising beyond others
Might feel like a win
But when you're alone
Success doesn't feel the same

Something out of your control
Changed your inner core
Now your starlight has dimmed
How do you continue your path

You're lonely in the sky
Even if everything seems fine
But the universe knows a star can rise above

WISH YOU WEREN'T HERE

There are times I wish
You were somebody I never met,
But you know it isn't true,
Even if I don't say it outright

You know how much I love
The drama that comes from you
You can always call my bluff

I'll never let your haunting voice go
In my mind, I can't remember
What you used to say to hurt me so,
But it isn't over yet, you could come back
Start everything back up again

DEEP DOWN INTO THE POND

Being pulled down into the pond
As if the plants have the life to pull
That's when everything feels heavy

You can't imagine what is going on
You're just scared to go under
And then the clutches unlatch
You breathe life back again

Suddenly, you're in another place
Back in time when you're needed most
That's when you realize that
Everything feels heavy for a reason
If you don't know what it is yet

WORDS NOT UNDERSTOOD

No one understood what made
My heart turned into dry leaves
Beside the pond filled with
Untouched magic
Until we arrived there

I was forgotten by the world
Frozen as a stone by ice
I wanted to let go of the pain
But my mind chose to be
The bird that repeated itself
Words that no one understood

SICK AND TIRED

I've been sick for so long
I don't know what normal is
I've given myself heartache so much
I don't know what falling in love is
I've been tired for so long
I don't know what to do
I've driven the roads you taught me
Because I need to easy way to go
But I'm tired of telling people why
I loved you when you made me cry
Ignoring me for far too long
But I'm tired, so I won't let you go
Even if you've moved on
To someone you always wanted

FROZEN FATE

What if I were stuck frozen
Within the pond? Would that be
My final fate? Or would you
Find me in another way?

I'm waiting, not quite paralyzed yet
But you'll find me soon
As the main attraction

Just like the man who
Adventured through a cave
With great expectations
Never quite finding a way out
Truly paralyzed by stones

Long lost, but never forgotten
The pond is now the main attraction
Will it remain there forever
Just like the feelings I have
That will never let me go

TENGO MIEDO DE PERDER

Tengo miedo pero no puedo hacer nada
Perdí la oportunidad al encontrar a el
El otro que puede ser mi corazón
Tengo miedo que sea muy tarde
Nunca voy a poder encontrar a el
Pero puedo ver a el en mi sueños
Está aquí conmigo para siempre y nunca
Cuando yo despierte todos las mañanas
Tengo miedo que esta vez no pueda
Dormir con la mente y corazón perdido
Una adentro de una caverna de una montaña
Y la otra adentro de el estanque del bosque
Las dos son mi pasión perdida para siempre
Porque tengo miedo de perder a ti y yo

NEW DAY EMERGING

Hope is a new day emerging ahead
If only we could hope all the time
We can stare at the pond for hours
We'll see life taking its turns each day

Just like the turtles hesitate to appear
No matter what, they're drawn to find
Their survival and their desire to be nearby
Before they dive into the depths below

These turtles don't know what is ahead
But they emerge from the depths of water
Knowing that there will be tomorrow
That is what we must do with hope
Even if we don't feel like it

DRAMATIC PASSION

I want to slap him like a dame in the movies
Just when he gets on my nerves
While knowing he will never hit me back
I want to feel like I can defend myself
But it's all dramatized in the cinema
Like a moment when everyone watches
Pull the arrow away from the bow

How can we find the physical passion?
Without causing pain to either of us
It's like pausing a car crash before it hits
It's a simple desire to walk towards the pond
Like I'm feeling power flow within me
I want to be reminded that my heart is still there

IMAGINING A BRIGHTER DAY

Some days, I imagine myself
As I wish I could be, a full-time writer
She spends her days writing her books
Finding times to sketch out her daily life
Where there are little messages left behind
By a warm tea cup from her husband
Before he leaves for his daily work
The flow of words breaks down
As soon as a distant cry starts
But it's the break she needs
As she sees her baby's smile
She and her baby wait for him
To return home to celebrate the day
A moment of three together is the best
But I know it's all part of my imagination

WILL I FIND THAT LOVE?

I wish I could believe in that love
Where someone will be my partner
We'll make moves together
I haven't found that partner
Even if there are options
Maybe I'm alone at the pond
Haunting like a ghost indefinitely
Bitter and scornful of the ones
Who made me lose time with them
Instead of finding the right one
Or will he find me like an adventure
He just hasn't reached me yet
I'm losing hope that he will arrive
Maybe he will be disappointed
That I'm broken without repair
Children will never arrive from me
All because of a lifesaving treatment

SWIPE MY MIND

I don't know how to let go
I have held on to everything
That's what I've been told
It isn't true, I have discarded
Like the changes of seasons
Every time emotions take hold
In a total breakdown, I push away
As if a spell to swipe my mind
Of the many pages of history and
Every desire that has been denied
I would rather weave the spell to swipe my mind
To forget those who were never mine
And the disease that changed everything

PERDIENDO LA ESPERANZA

La esperanza is always needed
Revolución comes from la esperanza
We can't move forward without it
When we want change, it comes first
Within, but how do we do that

La esperanza viene de los mejores
Momentos del pasado que no puedes olvidar
We can ponder and reflect on those momentos
But la esperanza is harder to find than ever
When el mundo has broken down

We break ourselves apart
We put ourselves together
When we break la esperanza
We lose more than ever before

PERDIENDO LA PACIENCIA

Just be patient, that's what they say
Why can't I make a magic potion
You'll arrive where I am by the pond
Or would jumping in change my fate
Will the pond take me where you are?
I've been patient for far too long

I expected you to be in chemotherapy,
Last ditch hope in radiation therapy,
As if you had cancer, too, we would
Fight the disease together, just like
My favorite characters but our fate
Would be that we survive, but broken
Not able to make a family of our own

Even my mind can't find that happy ending
Even if we crashed and burned
I know I shouldn't wish cancer
On my worst enemy and my lover
But I can't find my mind anywhere else

I'LL ALWAYS BE THERE

Oh, say you'll be there
As we jump into the pond
Traveling through time to when
Being a girl was all about dancing for fun
And our whole life was ahead of us

While there's still so much life left
I still want to feel like that when
Pain in my life has come from
More than heartaches and
Regrets of missing out on
What it means to be a woman

A mother, a wife, and everything successful
In her life's pursuit of her passions
Maybe I have that last one
Because I've given all of myself
I swear I'll always be there
But maybe not how you want me

AM I A GOOD FRIEND?

I want to believe chemotherapy broke
Everything about me, but I was already
Broken before chemo entered my veins
Not just the typical heartaches, but
Also, the friends I thought I could trust
But I know they wouldn't say it, so I will

I know I wasn't a good friend to you
If I were, maybe we would still be friends
I know I wasn't a good friend to you
If I were, we would never have been friends
I keep those feelings to a minimum
Everyone is at a distance now

I thought we learned the lesson
That we're all connected now
But we went back to our busy lives
Now we're just waiting for the right time
To say hello and goodbye, or nothing at all

BURN IT AWAY

Burn what no longer serves us
Never settle for the middle
We must start anew
We've accomplished more
Than what we have imagined
Let us rise like a phoenix
Time after time
We've destroyed what once was
For the present and the future
Begins as we rise into the night
It's a relief when we burn
What no longer serves

MAGICAL CHANGE ENERGY

I am constantly changing, but you don't see it
I am like the tree leaves near the pond
Throughout the year, but you don't notice
If you did, the changes would happen the same way

I grow with each passion that I find
Until the Texas drought comes back
Where I wither away from your damages
Eventually, I grow again with seasonal rains

That led me to whatever passion
I need the most until the drought comes
Don't worry about me, I have what I need
The pond is there like a constant companion
That contains my magical energy for change

FEARLESS WITH YOU

I've always desired powers
My good side says to be a superhero
My wicked side says to be a witch
Either way, I want to be fearless
I can do anything possible
I want to stop feeling powerless
I want to not fear falling
Or is it failing to reach you
I know there's a wall between
If you knew me, you would know
I could be fearless with you
I wouldn't care about getting hurt
As long as I could be everything for you
Maybe I don't want powers
Only be fearless with you
If only you could find me
Besides this local pond
While you're far across the pond

MY VOICE MUST ECHO

Jumping into a pond
is like an unexplored cave
It looks smaller at first glance
Then, as you get deeper
It's much more than you
Unlike a cave, my voice can't echo
As we fall deeper into the water
Until I can emerge from the surface
So do what I can to stay afloat
Because my voice is meant for more
It needs to be heard like an unexplored cave

PROUD OF WHO I'VE BECOME

I can't perform eight times a day,
But I found the pacing meant for me,
I've learned that I have talent,
But it takes a different approach,
I know that I am not the trauma,
Of all the hurt I have been put through,
I am the independent black cat
Wandering the local wilderness
And I know how to make a difference

IT'S WHO I AM

The silence on the pond waters,
The pain as the leaves fall away,
The determination of ducks gliding toward
The handsome, unexpecting stranger,

Because of you, I wanted
Dangerous men to thrill me
Who expected a slap back
Now I want to get you back
Even if it takes us to the past
Where we can't take anything back

You were the one in the mirror
Owed me some time ago
When I turn, you're not there
Now is the time for my female rage
Don't believe me? You'll see
I am the witch by the pond
And the Goddess by the wild, wide sea

Drawings in this book were made by Christina Vourcos

ACKNOWLEDGEMENTS

This book wouldn't exist without my fellow writers. As I mentioned in the beginning of this book, the TV show writers for THE WAY HOME created the idea of a time-traveling pond. I knew of a local pond nearby. So I thought it would be interesting to explore reflecting on the past, as if jumping into the time-traveling pond, but the only thing I could impact wouldn't be the past, but the present.

I thought about my heartache, including dealing with fighting lymphoma, and how it has impacted me. I thought it would work so well for my next poetry book. To give myself a bit of creative distance, I started the book with the idea of the Witch beside the pond, instructing me of what to share. There is also myth of a witch by the pond in THE WAY HOME too, but different than what I did for my book. I hope that this creative perspective led to some kind of impact in your life because I know it brought unexpected healing for me.

Those writers weren't the only ones that inspired my writing for this book. I have to thank fellow poet Whitney Hanson and her journal IN POETRY WE SAY for sparking some interesting poems that I would have never explored otherwise through her journal prompts that I made uniquely mine as my mind thought of bitter responses like a witch with vengeance but she is truly good inside. A few other poets have inspired me with their journals and creative prompts such as Flor Ana's NOURISH YOUR TEMPLE: Self -Love & Care Poetry Journal, IN-Q & Passion Planner's THE NEVER ENDING NOW POETRY JOURNAL, Shelby Leigh's SMALL STEPS TO SELF-LOVE journal, Amanda Lovelace's BELIEVE IN YOUR OWN MAGIC oracle deck, Anastasia Lindsey's OCEAN & WILD FIRE poetry decks.

Additionally, Austin Kleon's STEAL LIKE AN ARTIST, SHOW YOUR WORK, and KEEP GOING nonfiction books which made me realize how important journals could be for writers and poets, especially ones who want to go beyond words and illustrate. Which led me to read the nonfiction book WRITERS AND THEIR NOTEBOOKS, edited by Diana M. Raab, which has essays filled with explorations of how writers have found inspiration through different ways they use their notebooks. I also read WE NEED YOUR ART by Amie McNee, which supported

Austin Kleon's ideas of not limiting yourself to just writing words and much more.

I've always been interested in all kinds of art, but I found during my fight with lymphoma (starting December 2022 through the rest of 2023) that I needed creativity more than ever, but I struggled at times to find the words. Sometimes that meant that I needed to explore my creativity beyond words. While I've studied photography, I find that impactful in its own way, I noticed that drawing and painting added something more when I needed it the most. I still feel like I'm recovering from my fight with lymphoma, and I might always will, but I'm thankful to find resources that have helped me tap into my creativity. Including sketchbooks.

Recently when I started reading Samantha Dion Baker's books (DRAW YOUR DAY and DRAW YOUR WORLD), I knew it was just the inspiration I needed to be creative with what I had around me. I picked up Samantha's DRAW YOUR DAY sketchbook and her prompts led me to see my world a bit differently. I wasn't worried about perfection, but trying my best to draw and paint what I noticed or what I wanted to create on the page. Sometimes I didn't use the prompts, but I used her strategies in her books and her newsletter to sketch what was inspiring me, such as the local pond. She led me to find new art supplies, like watercolor pencils. While you can't see their effect in this book, you can find my updates through social media and my newsletter that show how colorful they can be. But the drawings wouldn't have come to be without Samantha's influence.

I also want to thank Shelby Leigh for not only her latest journal and poetry books, but also her Creative's Content Club. This club is for marketing support for creatives, including authors. She has taught me so much about writing, marketing, and provided support to share my work when it felt overwhelming. I've also connected to fellow authors through this club and beyond because of her.

Additionally, I want to thank Racquel Henry, her writing studio Writer's Atelier, and her literary magazine Black Fox. While I haven't been accepted into Black Fox, one of the submission periods inspired a bit of my poetry. It also was one of the moments that made me realize while I could still be independent in publishing my books. I could still submit poems to literary magazines. Eventually, this same year, I submitted to a local literary magazine Windward Review and received acceptance. Since 2024, Writer's Atelier has a writing challenge, that I've been involved in, called Write Brave Challenge. The Fall and Spring editions have helped me complete many poems in this book. I appreciate all the support that the challenge provided. There's many authors, poets, and creatives that I would love to thank as well, but I hope you know that you've inspired me more than you know.

I want to thank all those who have supported my indie author career so far and who will in the future. I wouldn't be able to provide these books without you. This includes my friends (such as Jennifer Lyn), fellow colleagues at TAMUCC, and my family. Most of all, all who have read my books. Your support has made a difference. I will keep writing and publishing for you. I hope you will continue to share your support with me through any way you can, from purchasing books, sharing your thoughts online, telling others about my books, supporting on social media and through my newsletter. I hope you will continue to leave reviews on Amazon because not only do I appreciate your feedback, it helps future readers find my books.

PRAISE FOR AUTHOR

DIVE WITHIN Poetry book reviews:

"Poignant yet uplifting"
"Powerful and moving book! A MUST READ"
"Poetry that helps a reader heal"
"A honest collection"
"A thoughtful read for anyone with cancer
or loves someone who is."

- AMAZON FIVE STAR BOOK REVIEWERS

WRITING MATTERS AND SO DO YOU Nonfiction book reviews:

"The title of the book says it all!"
"Inspiring"
"Helpful content"
"This book was meant to be in my hands!"

- AMAZON FIVE STAR BOOK REVIEWERS

NEVER FORGET book blurbs:

"Don't miss out on this story rich in Latino culture!" - Christina Farley,

ABOUT THE AUTHOR

Christina Vourcos

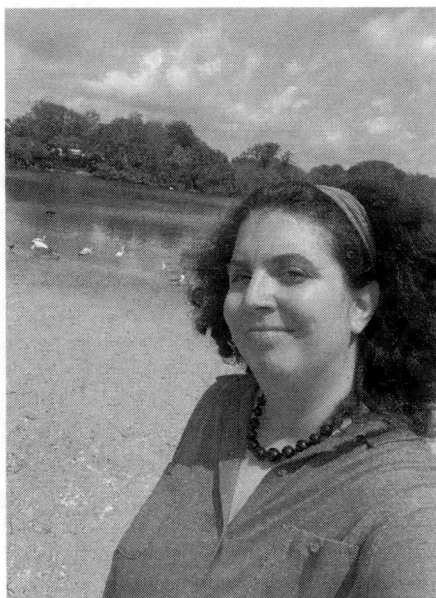

Author of the poetry book DIVE WITHIN, Christina Vourcos has been inspired to publish independently her books ranging from fiction, poetry, and nonfiction. Thanks to her degrees in Literature, including a Masters, and her Journalism background, she is able to. She is also an English adjunct instructor at Texas A&M University - Corpus Christi and works as website content manager for Jeremy-Jordan.com

As a Greek Latina growing up in Texas, especially South Texas, being bilingual with Spanish since childhood has been a superpower, and wants to be trilingual in Greek. Additionally, Christina is a lymphoma survivor. Learn more about her books and subscribe to her free newsletter through her website: authorchristinavourcos.com

BOOKS BY THIS AUTHOR

Dive Within: Poetry On Fighting Lymphoma And Mental Health

Writing Matters And So Do You: Writing With A Mental Health Focus

Never Forget: Latinx Scifi Mystery College Romance Novel

Untitled Poetry Book (Coming Soon)

Made in the USA
Monee, IL
13 June 2025

f91bf22d-35d4-46ee-baaa-63405e8bfeeeR02